UNLEASHING
Of
Supernatural
Miracles
And
Unexplainable
Blessings

By: Sharon Hall - Green

Dedication

I dedicate this book to my parents, the people who have been my greatest example of the love of Christ. Your pureness behind closed doors when no one could see, but us, showed me what true holiness was. You lived what you preached. You helped me remain humble; making sure I never got a big head with the gifts God gave me.

You instilled humbleness and righteousness.
Thank you, Mom and Dad. I love you and am forever grateful. You taught me to praise God in all things, and the results have produced so many miracles and supernatural blessings in my life.

I love you dearly, and
I pray this makes you proud!

books may be ordered through booksellers or by
contacting:

Shay Ministries
3226 Norwich Street
Brunswick, GA 31520

The views expressed in this work are solely those
of the author,
Sharon Hall-Green
Any illustration provided by iStock and such
images are being used for illustrative purposes.

Printed in the United States Of America

CONTENT

I prophesy to you that after reading this book and grabbing hold of the principles, YOU WILL BEGIN TO CLIMB! Just as you see the steps on a ladder, each will take you higher and higher. The more you apply the simple principles found in this book, the more they will become a part of you and become your lifestyle. You will be a living testimony and live a supernatural life of favor. You will live what the bible speaks of in Amos 9:13, *"Things are going to happen so fast, your head will swim. One thing fast on the heels of the other".* God works by principles, and as you learn them, you will begin to tap into a supernatural flow of miracles and blessings that will PUSH you forward in every area of your life. It is your time to obtain what is rightfully yours. Your delay is over now! Get ready to CLIMB! Get ready for everything that has been TIED UP to be UNLEASHED!

It was not by chance you picked up this book. It was destined for you to read it at this exact moment. TIME IS UP! Open your mouth and declare it: Time is up. I'm unleashing every blessing in my life that has been held by the enemy or that has not been claimed, because of not being in the right position. God has blessings with your name on it, and He wants you to rise and possess them. He has commanded blessings upon thee. However, there are many adversaries who fight your manifestation! (Deut. 2:24; Deut. 2:28 1 Cor. 16:9). You have the power to unleash the blessings of God. You must use one of the greatest weapons you have and invoke a divine intervention, which is PRAISE. Praise is a genuine way to experience supernatural miracles and unexplainable blessings. Praise is the weapon that can UNLEASH, UNLOCK, and

BUST LOOSE all your stuff! If you have tried everything else, why not try PRAISE, "PUT A PRAISE ON IT!" Praise has worked supernatural miracles in my life. The very things the doctors said I would not do, I am doing. I have learned to praise God even when it is a "sacrifice." I remember times: I would cry all day and ask God why me. I hated that I could not take care of my children, and that could not walk and my new legs were wheels. Then one day, I heard a voice say: do you trust me? PRAISE ME. From that day on, (NO, it was not easy) I praised God, some days good and some days not so good. However, Praise started changing things! The more I praised him, the more I saw him work! Now, your situation may be different but *Praise specializes in fighting battles...* whatever your battle is... It is READY TO HANDLE IT!

ARE YOU READY? Let's Go!

2 Chronicles 20:17-18, 21-22

*17 Ye shall not need to fight in this battle: **set yourselves,** stand ye still, and see the salvation of the LORD with you, O Judah and Jerusalem: fear not, nor be dismayed; tomorrow go out against them: for the LORD will be with you. 18 And Jehoshaphat bowed his head with his face to the ground: and all Judah and the inhabitants of Jerusalem fell before the LORD, worshipping the LORD. 21 And when he had consulted with the people, he appointed singers unto the Lord, and that should praise the beauty of holiness, as they went out before the army, and to say, Praise the Lord; for his mercy endureth forever. 22 And when they began to sing and to praise, the LORD set ambushments against the children of Amon, Moab, and mount Seir, which were come against Judah; and they were smitten.* According to 2 Chronicles 20:17-18, 21-22, God has already given you the PROMISE of VICTORY that you will not have to fight this battle! He gives the conclusion before He gives the instructions. Why? Because He wants you

8

to know that HE'S GOT YOU. God wants to build your faith and trust in Him first. Like a good father, God wants his children to feel safe and protected. God wants you to know that you have nothing to fear or worry about. When I was a little girl, I always felt safe whenever my father was around, no matter the situation. God loves you even more than your natural father. Therefore, He wants you to know that no matter who or what you are up against, the battle is not yours. It is His, and the fight is fixed. **You have already won before it even starts.** God just wants you to have faith in Him. God always keeps His promises, and He will fulfill them in your life. Hebrews 10:23 comforts us, God can be trusted to keep his promises. Prepare yourself. The arrival of your manifestation is soon to come!

PRINCIPLE 1 - SET YOURSELVES

[17] Ye shall not need to fight in this battle: **set yourselves...**The definition of the word *set* means to place, position, lay or deposit. I am going to deal with two words: POSITION and DEPOSIT. These two words brought forth a whole new meaning for me. Let's first look at the word, *position.* Position yourselves means to get in the right place to receive. As a young girl, I would love to play in the water sprinklers. However, they would rotate in a wild circle. I had to position myself in the perfect spot to get soaking wet. If I was NOT IN THAT spot, the sprinkler would pass over me every time or only a part of my body would get wet. This is the same way with God. We must position ourselves so that we will not miss our blessings or receive the partial manifestation of what God has promised us. Now, let's deal with the word, *deposit.* Whenever a person is paid

from their place of employment, they will often take their paycheck to the bank to make a deposit. We deposit our checks in the bank because we believe it to be a **safe place** for our funds. However, we don't know any of the staff at the bank or what they will do with our money once it is deposited. Nevertheless, we just TRUST them. God whispered to me and said, "Shay, the banks get more trust than me." No questions asked, no grumbling or complaining. Then he said, "Deposit yourself?" I knew exactly what he was saying. He wanted me to trust him with depositing my life before him. He is our SAFE PLACE, where we can drop off all our cares and leave them there. However, we often want to make withdrawals from our heavenly accounts, without first making a deposit. Just like in the natural, if you do not make a deposit, you cannot make a withdrawal. In Luke 12:48,

For unto whomsoever much is given, of him shall much be required; God requires us to SET OURSELVES. This is our preparation for the blessing; there MUST BE A DEPOSIT!

PRINCIPLE 1. SUMMARY

Setting yourself is vital. This is why God mentioned it first. You can't miss this step! For us to partake in Ephesians 1:3 where it states, *"we have been blessed with every spiritual blessing in heavenly places in Christ,"* we must be in position to receive. No deposit. No withdrawal. In any sport, if a player is to make a winning play, he must be in the proper place to receive the ball. Set yourself before God today. Say *"God, I deposit myself before you, flaws and all. I trust you and your plan for my life. I surrender my will to your will. With childlike faith, I give you my hand. Lead me, and I will follow you!"*

HOW DO YOU POSITION or

DEPOSIT YOURSELF?

18 And Jehoshaphat bowed his head with his

face to the ground: and all Judah and the

inhabitants of Jerusalem fell before the LORD,

worshipping the LORD.

Jehoshaphat and all of Judah worshipped! Whenever you start worshipping, God will find you. You've been looking for Him, but if you just start worshipping, He will SEEK AFTER YOU. The bible says in John 4:23, *"But the hour cometh, and now is, when the true worshippers shall worship the Father in spirit and truth: for the Father seeketh such to worship him."* Do you see the word seeketh? This means he will seek for you. Worship is your position. Deposit yourselves before Him, and He will find you. Deposit is storing up something. In other words, you are making spiritual deposits every time you worship. How full or how empty is your heavenly account? The scripture says in Galatians 6:7-9 *Be not deceived; God is not mocked: for whatsoever a man soweth, that shall he also* *reap. For he that soweth to his flesh shall of the flesh reap corruption; but he that soweth to the Spirit shall of the Spirit reap life everlasting."*

What is in your account to withdraw? What you sow is what you will reap. If you deposit in the spirit, you reap in the spirit. If you sow in the flesh, you reap in the flesh. Remember your INPUT DETERMINES YOUR OUTPUT. There are two investments: A Flesh Investment and a Spirit Investment. Which one are you depositing into? Every time you pray, worship, and praise, you are making a spiritual deposit. Just as in the natural, if you keep making deposits, your account increases. Therefore, see it in the spirit; every time you deposit of prayer, praise, etc..., and your spiritual account increase. In Psalms 31:19, says Oh how great is your goodness, which you have STORE UP for them that fear you; which you have wrought for them

14

that trust in you before the sons of men! Your praise is not in vain; God is storing it up in your account. He will increase you more and more you (Psalms 115:14). Jehoshaphat and all of Judah made a worship deposit in the midst of their TRIAL. They knew that naturally, they could not win, but if they made a spiritual DEPOSIT, nothing would be impossible. Right now, take a few minutes and make a deposit. This will open the gate for your release. This spiritual release will give you a natural release.

PRINCIPLE 2 - STAND STILL

[17] *Ye shall not need to fight in this battle: set yourselves,* **stand ye still**...

Standing still is the principle we have the most problem with. We have the biggest fight here because we have our plans and agendas. We want God to go along with those plans. God has His plan for our lives, and we have to follow his lead. We struggle with the unknown. Often, we know the way we want to take, but most of the time with God, He leads us blindfolded until He's ready to reveal it. Do you remember what I was talking about earlier? Daddy, our heavenly father, wants us to simply trust him. He's got you!

The enemy knows you. He knows what you like. He knows you like details. He knows that you are worried and that you want answers and help. So, he will present what appears to be a way of "escape." This is just his trick to get you to

MOVE. He knows that when God doesn't come through when we want Him to, we won't STAND STILL; which will result in us trying to help God out. When we don't stand still, we end up worse than we were before. God wants you to TRUST Him like you do when you make your financial deposits at the bank. You drop your deposit off and leave, and you don't ask any questions. God said I've already told you the victory is yours. I've already made you a promise. Now, Trust me! STAND STILL. Relax and know that I am God. Know that I make good on my promises. I am a promise keeper. If I said it, it will come to pass!

Isaiah 55:11
*So shall my word be that goes forth out of my mouth: **it shall not return unto me void,** but it shall accomplish that which I please, **and it shall prosper in the thing for which I sent it.***

Number 23:19

God is not a man, that he should lie; *neither the son of man, that he should repent: hath he said, and shall he not do it?* **Or hath he spoken, and shall he not make it good?**

PRINCIPLE 2. SUMMARY

Standing still is a place where things seem to be put on hold. (It is the waiting room of life.) However, it is the opposite of God. You are standing still while God is busy at work. It is like when a woman is pregnant, it seems like nothing is happening, but on the inside, the baby is growing, changing, and developing. God says while you are waiting, I know you cannot SEE it but things are GROWING, CHANGING and DEVELOPING. The changes you've been feeling is God at work. Just stand still and don't move from this place. You are about to see the results of your deposit!

PRINCIPLE 3 – SEE THE SALVATION

[17] Ye shall not need to fight in this battle: set yourselves, stand ye still, and SEE the salvation of the LORD with you...

Problems will come that seem hopeless and impossible to the natural eye. What can you do? I want to encourage you to see the salvation of the Lord work on your behalf. Do not be moved by the situation. Nothing is impossible for God if you can only believe! (Mark 9:23) Look close at this; it is a command, not a statement. It says see. It commands you to SEE. In other words, have a spirit of expectancy. Look for it to happen. The definition of seeing is to look, view, discern. Salvation means to preserve or deliver from destruction, the act of saving. In other words, see God delivering or saving you from whatever state you are in! Right now, take 30 seconds and begin to visualize God delivering you from whatever situation you are in! Be in it as a movie. See, yourself not sad and lonely but

19

happy and living life with joy, see yourself no longer single but married in love and waking up to your spouse, or see your banking account not overdrawn but see yourself at the bank with a check for your desired amount. Whatever it is you want just SEE IT! 1 Samuel 12:16 declares, "Now then, stand still and see this great thing the LORD is about to do before your eyes!" Also, Proverbs, 23:7 says as he thinketh in his heart, so is he. You become what you believe. If you can SEE it, you can have it. I will give you all the land you SEE (Genesis 13:15). Your hater or enemy is not what limits you. Your limits come from the distance of your sight. God will give you as much or as little as you SEE. **You decide what you produce. *You cannot SEIZE what you cannot SEE!*** If you have the faith to SEE it, He will produce it! God will MIRROR what you SEE!

PRINCIPLE 3. SUMMARY

See the Salvation is one of the hardest principles to apply. It is to have faith and not fear. God wants us to expect that He is going to deliver us without a doubt. When you have a guarantee that a check or a package is in the mail, you look for it. (Without a doubt) You are waiting for it. God says, "I have given you a guarantee, all you have to do is look for it! IT IS ON THE WAY! You are too close to your blessing. Fear comes now to delay it. Push with faith. SEE me doing what I have promised in my word. You have a package on the way. Visualize it being delivered to your door. Lift up now thine eyes, and look from the place where (Genesis 13:14) you are and SEE it!

PRINCIPLE 4 – PRAISE

[22] *"And when they began to sing and to praise,* Jehoshaphat FOLLOWED INSTRUCTIONS and did what God told him. He *appointed singers unto the Lord that they should praise the beauty of holiness, as they went out before the army, and say, Praise the Lord; for his mercy endureth forever."* Now, I know this doesn't make any common sense, for the praisers to go out FIRST, who had NO PHYSICAL WEAPONS against the children of Amon, Moab, and Mount Seir, which were three great armies.

Why did God want PRAISE to go out first? What is in PRAISE that defeats the enemy? Can praise have that much power to defeat a battle of this magnitude? What happens is that praise causes God to fight for you. *He takes place in the battle while you watch on the sideline.* Have you ever watched a wrestling match and one of the fighters is getting beat up? Then another fighter has his hand out saying TAG ME IN! God is saying you will not have to fight at all in this battle if you just **"TAG ME IN"** with your praise. If you praise me, I will show up. PRAISE is a knock at the door that God will always open. Praise invokes His divine presence. Psalm 22:3 – "But thou art holy, *O thou that **inhabitest the praises of Israel.**"*

God comes and dwells and lives in praise. He cannot turn down an invitation to a Praise party. Why, because, God created us to give Him praise. Praise is like a magnet. God attaches Himself to us. Praise has such force that it draws a mighty God to a human being. Your praise will draw God to you. Open your mouth and praise him. Let him connect you.

PRINCIPLE 4. SUMMARY

Praise is powerful! It is like a magnet that draws God to you! When you praise, you attract God's presence. He cannot deny praise. He dwells in it Psalms 53:2 says, God looks down from heaven to see if any who seek him. The thing, I love about God is that he starts off looking down, but when he sees a praiser, he comes down. Praise causes a REACTION or RESPONSE out of God. Jeremiah 20:13 says Praise the Lord! He rescues the oppressed. When you praise, God will RESPOND! If you want to get *God's attention, becomes addicted to praise.* He is far from a person who complains and murmurs. In Psalms 106: 24-27 says they did not believe in His word, But grumbled in their tents; They did not listen to the voice of the LORD. Therefore He swore to them that he would cast them down in the wilderness. It is praise that gets God's attention. Take your mind off of your situation, regardless how bad it may look, and open your mouth and praise God. You are invoking his presence. He is looking down at you, and you are getting his attention. Your action RIGHT NOW is causing him to REACT (you can feel him if you allow him to consume this moment). You invited him, and he has shown up.

PRAISE BRINGS RESULTS

²² "And when they began to sing and to praise, the LORD set ambushments against the children of Amon, Moab, and Mount Seir, which were come against Judah; and they were smitten."

Look at the scripture. It says the Lord set ambushments against them. That means that GOD SHOWED UP ON THE SCENE. Praise released the battle off of them, and God was tagged in. Praise is the master key that gives us access to prayers being answered. It is not enough just to pray, but we must praise God. **You can pray amiss (James 4:3), But you can not Praise amiss.** You can have unanswered prayers, but you can not have unanswered praise. Praise brings the wonder-working power of God in our situation. The Bible says in *Exodus 15:11, "Who is like unto thee, O LORD, among the gods? Who is like thee, glorious in holiness, **fearful in praises, doing wonders?"*** Praise always gets results. **When you praise God, victory becomes your companion. It's like you become married to victory**. If you make praise a lifestyle, you will have a life of VICTORY. Praise always put GOD on the scene, and HE WILL do like a good father, STEP IN and go to work on your behalf. The reason the enemy cannot hold down a praiser is that they are always invoking God's presence in their situation. Are bad things going to happen? Yes. However, you must know how to counteract when they do. A weapon is useless not being used or partially. Also, it most cases a weapon must be used more than once. Praise is your weapon. Use it to full capacity and continually. Psalms 34:1 says, I will bless the Lord at all times: his praise shall continually be in my mouth. Defeat and praise will not stay in the same house. One has to leave! They hate each other. Praise evicts defeat, and victory moves in. Whenever your life is full of praise, supernatural miracles and blessings will happen unexplainably. When Paul and Silas were in jail, they prayed and sang praises, and suddenly the jail doors flew open, and **EVERYONE'S** chains were loose (Acts 16:25)! Your praise can open doors that seem impossible, and also set free those connected to you! *The wonders-working power of God comes when you praise.* **You want a wonder just praise!**

BENEFITS OF PRAISE

Causes Multiplication - (John 6:6-11)
Jesus gave thanks, and five loaves of bread and two fish multiplied supernaturally to feed five thousand men.

Awakens stubborn things - (John 11:40-44)
Jesus gave thanks, and Lazarus came out of the grave.

Reveals God's Master Key - (Rev 3:7) And to the angel of the church in Philadelphia write; These things saith he that is holy, he that is true, he that hath the key of David, he that openeth, and no man shutteth; and shutteth, and no man openeth.

The devil will go on the run - (Matt 4:10-11)
Jesus said to him, "Away from me, Satan! For it is written: 'Worship the Lord your God, and serve him only.' "
Then the devil left him, and angels came and attended him.

Causes Increase - (Psalm 67:5-7)

Let the people praise thee, O God; let all the people praise thee. [6] Then shall the earth yield her increase; and God, even our own God, shall bless us. [7] God shall bless us; and all the ends of the earth shall fear Him.

Restores Lost Blessings - (Daniel 4:36-37)

At the same time my reason returned unto me; and for the glory of my kingdom, mine honour and brightness returned unto me; and my counselors and my lords sought unto me; and I was established in my kingdom, and excellent majesty was added unto me.

[37] Now I Nebuchadnezzar praise and extol and honour the King of heaven, all whose works are truth, and his ways judgment: and those that walk in pride he is able to abase.

Opens Hard Cases - (Acts 16:25-26)

25 And at midnight Paul and Silas prayed, and sang praises unto God: and the prisoners heard them.26 And suddenly there was a great earthquake, so that the foundations of the prison

were shaken: and immediately all the doors were opened, and every one's bands were loosed.

Manifests the Anointing- (Psalm 89:20)
I have found David my servant; with my holy oil have I anointed him:

Silences Opposition- (Ps 8:2 NIV)
Through the praise of children and infants you have established a stronghold against your enemies, to silence the foe and the avenger.

Blessing is preserved - (Ecclesiastes 3:14)
I know that, whatsoever God doeth, it shall be forever: nothing can be put to it, nor any thing taken from it: and God doeth it, that men should fear before him.

Deliver the needy from hand of evil doers - (Jeremiah 20:13)
Sing to the LORD, praise the LORD! For He has delivered the soul of the needy one From the hand of evildoers.

WHAT HAPPENS WHEN YOU DON'T PRAISE

You turn your Blessings into Curses

Malachi 2:2   -² If ye will not hear, and if ye will not lay it to heart, to give glory unto my name, saith the LORD of hosts, I will even send a curse upon you, and I will curse your blessings: yea, I have cursed them already, because ye do not lay it to heart.

2 "And now this indictment, you priests! If you refuse to obediently listen, and if you refuse to honor me, GOD-of-the-Angel-Armies, in worship, then I'll put you under a curse. I'll exchange all your blessings for curses. In fact, the curses are already at work because you're not serious about honoring me. Yes and the curse will extend to your children. I'm going to plaster your faces with rotting garbage, garbage thrown out from your feasts. That's what you have to look forward to!

31

I will stop blessing those that grumble

Numbers 14:26-29

26 And the LORD spake unto Moses and unto Aaron, saying, 27 How long shall I bear with this evil congregation, which murmur against me? I have heard the murmurings of the children of Israel, which they murmur against me.

28 Say unto them, As truly as I live, saith the LORD, as ye have spoken in mine ears, so will I do to you:

29 Your carcasses shall fall in this wilderness; and all that were numbered of you, according to your whole number, from twenty years old and upward which have murmured against me.

TRY this and watch God move miraculously:

Create a lifestyle of gratitude. When you are thankful, you open your life up to a continual flow of signs and wonders. **Your gratitude determines your altitude! THIS IS HOW YOU CLIMB!** The bible says in 1Thessalonians 5:18, "In everything, give thanks: for this is the will of God in Christ Jesus concerning you." He said in everything, give thanks. Stop right now and find things to be thankful for. Name things and tell Him thank you. Now, this is (his WILL), and since this is (his WILL) He is obligated to fulfill the promises connected to the WILL!

Well, you say it is easy to be thankful when everything is going good, or when God is blessing you. But, it's not so easy when nothing is working out right or when life hits you with a hard blow that knocks the wind from you. We ask ourselves: How can I be thankful for this?

33

This verse is saying to be thankful IN all situations. When you look at the original Hebrew word for IN that is used here, it means "during" or "in the middle of." Therefore, no matter what comes your way in life you are to be thankful in the middle of it.

Let's Practice. Start thanking Him. FIRST STEP: Name things that are good in your life and tell him thank you, also the things that aren't so good. For example, my friend and her children were in a car accident, and a deer hit the side of her vehicle and tore off the front of the car as a result of the impact. However, everyone made it out alive. The car can be replaced! Now, the accident wasn't a good thing, but I told her to praise and thank God because she and her kids were spared. God is still so good! Another example, a lady was having problems on the job. Every day it was one thing after another. They eventually fired her. I told her to thank God for the time she had on that job, for the pay she received from that job, I said thank him for being a provider in the midst of not having a job. Thank him for opening a door greater than what she had. I told her every time it crossed her mind and wanted to make her sad begin to praise. It was less than a week; she got a call from a job she had applied for months prior. They hired her with more money and less stress.

No, you may not be where you want, and yes it may be an ugly situation, but it could have been worse. There is someone, somewhere who is longing to be in your shoes. Yes, your shoes; as tight as they may feel RIGHT NOW. You are not thanking Him for the bad; you are thanking Him because, in the midst of it all, his love lasts forever (Psalm 106:1), God is still good (1

Chronicles 16:34), He is a God that answers (2 Timothy 2:13).

SECOND STEP - Begin thanking Him for what He is about to do. I know you haven't received the manifestation yet. However, this is where you trust and know that Daddy will come through for you. Tell Him, "God, I don't know how you're going to do it, but I thank you for...my new job making 75,000 a year. I thank you for saving my son, whom I have not seen in 5 years and reuniting him with his family." Declare by faith what you believe to see manifest in your life. *Remember, your thank you today determines your blessings tomorrow.* If someone you bless today is not grateful, then when it's time to bless them again, you are limited to how you want to bless them. However, when someone is thankful, you don't mind blessing them again. **GRATITUDE attracts more of its kind**. The more you are thankful for something; it's like a force that draws more of it to you. If you are thankful for the dollar, it will draw more of its kind. God brings interest and multiplication, so it comes back more! This is why it is important to have a thankful heart.

Thanksgiving and Praise are in the same family. When you start thanking God, it will produce praise, which invokes divine presence. God shows up. God sees it as a good thing when you thank and praise him. – (Psalms 92:1) – *"It is a good thing to give thanks unto the LORD, and to sing praises unto thy name, O most High."* Philippians 4:6 says, *"Be careful for nothing; but in everything by prayer and supplication with thanksgiving let your requests be made known unto God."* Praying is vitally important. It is how we commune with God. However, the angels attend to our prayer, but PRAISE brings God directly to you! Angels come when we pray. When Jesus prayed in the Garden of Gethsemane, angels appeared from heaven and gave strength to Jesus (Luke 22:43). When Zechariah prayed, an angel came. When Daniel prayed, Gabriel, the angel came with his answer. However, when you praise, God will show up on the scene. David was the only man who was noted as "a man after God's own heart" (Acts 13:22). David was a worshipper. He would dance with all of his might before the Lord, withholding nothing. He knew the importance of prayer, so he prayed three times a day. "Evening, and morning, and at noon, will I pray, and cry aloud: and he shall hear my voice" (Psalm 55:17). He touched God's heart with his praise! He would praise God seven times a day. *"Seven times a day do I praise thee because of thy righteous judgments."* (Psalm 119:164). He praised more than he prayed. You can touch God's heart with your praise! Praise God at all times, and as you do, it is going to work on your behalf.

You have tried other things, why not try praise. If praise can fight a battle without a weapon and open jail doors without a key, why not TRY IT, and see if it can WORK for you! It has the power to turn things around. God wants you to praise him so he can STEP IN. Victory is yours! Why fight or struggle if you don't have too? **You have all you need to win IN YOUR MOUTH!** *The power is in your tongue (*Prov.18:20) Your body may get worn out and weary, but your tongue never gets tired. Open your mouth and PRAISE him and he will move! Get ready for a LIFE OF VICTORY after VICTORY! Miracle after Miracle! Supernatural and unexplainable blessings!

15 Days of Praise &Thanksgiving Journal
Habakkuk 2:2
**And the LORD answered me, and said, write the vision,
and make it plain upon tables, that he may
run that readeth it.**

*It is stated that keeping a gratitude journal
will increase your
happiness, well-being, and income.*

DAY 1

"It is a good thing to give thanks unto the Lord, and to sing praises unto thy name, O Most High: To shew forth thy lovingkindness in the morning, and thy faithfulness every night" Psalm 92:1-2

Morning Thanksgiving (Name things you are thankful for)

_____

_____

_____

Pray: Lord, I thank you for waking me up this morning. I thank you for covering my family in your wings. I thank you for your favor. Today, I am thanking you for _____. I know that you can do all things, but fail! I will forever give your name the praise. In Jesus name, Amen.

Evening Thanksgiving (Thank him for what he has done today)

_____

_____

_____

_____

Take 5 minutes and just praise/worship him

Prayer Request or Praise Report Log

41

DAY 2

"Enter into his gates with thanksgiving, and into his courts with praise: be thankful unto him, and bless his name." Psalm 100:4

Morning Thanksgiving (Name things you are thankful for)

_____

_____

_____

Pray: Lord, I thank you for waking me up this morning. I thank you for all your many blessings. Renew my mind. Today, I am thanking you for _____. I know that you can do all things, but fail! I will forever give your name the praise. In Jesus name, Amen.

Evening Thanksgiving (Thank him for what he has done today)

_____

_____

_____

_____

Take 5 minutes and just praise/worship him

Prayer Request or Praise Report Log

DAY 3

"Continue in prayer, and watch in the same with thanksgiving" Colossians 4:2

Morning Thanksgiving (Name things you are thankful for)

_____

_____

_____

Pray: Lord, I thank you for waking me up this morning. I thank you for guiding me today. I thank you for your peace of mind in all situations. I thank you that nothing will disturb my joy today. I will smile and be happy today. I am thanking you for _____. I will forever give your name the praise. In Jesus name, Amen.

Evening Thanksgiving (Thank Him for what he has done today)

_____

_____

_____

_____

Take 5 minutes and just praise/worship him

Prayer Request or Praise Report Log

DAY 4

"O give thanks unto the LORD; for he is good; for his mercy endureth for ever." *1 Chronicles 16:34*

Morning Thanksgiving (Name things you are thankful for)

_____

_____

_____

Pray: Lord, I thank you for waking me up this morning. Help me to embrace anything that comes my way as an opportunity to see you at work. I thank you that when people see me they will see you. Today, I am thanking you for _____. I will forever give your name the praise. In Jesus name, Amen.

Evening Thanksgiving (Thank him for what he has done today)

_____

_____

_____

_____

Take 5 minutes and just praise/worship him

Prayer Request or Praise Report Log

DAY 5

"Be careful for nothing; but in every thing by prayer and supplication with thanksgiving let your requests be made known unto God." Philippians 4:6

Morning Thanksgiving (Name things you are thankful for)

_____

_____

_____

Pray: Lord, I thank you for waking me up this morning. I thank you for your protection. I thank you for unity in my home. I thank you for prosperity and favor. Today, I am thanking you for _____. I know that you can do all things, but fail! I will forever give your name the praise. In Jesus name, Amen.

Evening Thanksgiving (Thank him for what he has done today)

_____

_____

_____

_____

Take 5 minutes and just praise/worship him
Prayer Request or Praise Report Log

DAY 6

"O Come, let us sing for joy to the Lord; Let us shout joyfully to the rock of our salvation. Let us come into his presence with thanksgiving; let us make a joyful noise to him with songs of praise! For the Lord is a great God, and a great King above all gods." Ps. 95:1-3

Morning Thanksgiving (Name things you are thankful for)

_____

_____

_____

Pray: Lord, I thank you for waking me up this morning. I thank you for life, health, and strength. I thank you for joy and peace on today. Today, I am thanking you for _____. I know that you love me, and I will forever give your name the praise. In Jesus name, Amen.

Evening Thanksgiving (Thank him for what he has done today)

_____

_____

_____

_____

Take 5 minutes and just praise/worship him
Prayer Request or Praise Report Log

46

DAY 7

"I will give thanks to you, LORD, with all my heart; I will tell of all your wonderful deeds." Ps. 9:1

Morning Thanksgiving (Name things you are thankful for)

_____

_____

_____

Pray: Lord, I thank you for waking me up this morning. I thank you for another beautiful day. I thank you for wisdom and understanding as I face things today. I thank you for opening doors of opportunities. Today, I am thanking you for _____. I will forever give your name the praise. In Jesus name, Amen.

Evening Thanksgiving (Thank him for what he has done today)

_____

_____

_____

_____

Take 5 minutes and just praise/worship him

Prayer Request or Praise Report Log

DAY 8

"Giving thanks always and for everything to God the Father in the name of our Lord Jesus Christ,"
Eph. 5:20

Morning Thanksgiving (Name things you are thankful for)

_____

_____

_____

Pray: Lord, I thank you for waking me up this morning. I thank you for being so good to me. I thank you for ordering my steps and giving me patience to follow as you lead. Today, I am thanking you for _____. I will forever give your name the praise. InJesus name, Amen.

Evening Thanksgiving (Thank him for what he has done today)

_____

_____

_____

_____

Take 5 minutes and just praise/worship him

Prayer Request or Praise Report Log

DAY 9

"I will praise the name of God with song, and shall magnify Him with thanksgiving." Ps. 69:30

Morning Thanksgiving (Name things you are thankful for)

_____

_____

_____

Pray: Lord, I thank you for waking me up this morning. I thank you for covering under your wings. I thank you for blessing us with your favor. Today, I am thanking you for _____. I will forever give your name the praise. In Jesus name, Amen.

Evening Thanksgiving (Thank him for what he has done today)

_____

_____

_____

_____

Take 5 minutes and just praise/worship him

Prayer Request or Praise Report Log

DAY 10

"I will praise the name of God with song, and shall magnify Him with thanksgiving." Ps. 69:30

Morning Thanksgiving (Name things you are thankful for)

_____

_____

_____

Pray: Lord, I thank you for waking me up this morning. I thank you for renewing my heart your love. I thank you for blessing us with your favor. Today, I am thanking you for _____. I will forever give your name the praise. In Jesus name, Amen.

Evening Thanksgiving (Thank him for what he has done today)

_____

_____

_____

_____

Take 5 minutes and just praise/worship him

Prayer Request or Praise Report Log

DAY 11

"Let them give thanks to the LORD for His lovingkindness, And for His wonders to the sons of men! For He has satisfied the thirsty soul, and the hungry soul He has filled with what is good." Psalm 107:8-9

Morning Thanksgiving (Name things you are thankful for)

_____

_____

_____

Pray: Lord, I thank you for waking me up this morning. Lord, thank you peace of mind and strength to endure anything that I face today. I thank you for your wisdom. Today, I am thanking you for _____. I will forever give your name the praise. In Jesus name, Amen.

Evening Thanksgiving (Thank him for what he has done today)

_____

_____

_____

_____

Take 5 minutes and just praise/worship him

Prayer Request or Praise Report Log

DAY 12

"Sing to the LORD with thanksgiving; Sing praises to our God on the lyre, Who covers the heavens with clouds, Who provides rain for the earth, Who makes grass to grow on the mountains. He gives to the beast its food, And to the young ravens which cry."
Psalm 147:7-9

Morning Thanksgiving (Name things you are thankful for)

_____

_____

_____

Pray: Lord, I thank you for waking me up this morning. I thank you for your faithfulness and loving kindness towards me. I thank you for where I am weak you are strong, and daily I am becoming more like you. Today, I am thanking you for _____. I will forever give your name the praise. In Jesus name, Amen.

Evening Thanksgiving (Thank him for what he has done today)

_____

_____

_____

_____

Take 5 minutes and just praise/worship him
Prayer Request or Praise Report Log

52

DAY 13

*"Let us come before His presence with thanksgiving,
Let us shout joyfully to Him with psalms."*
Psalm 95:2

Morning Thanksgiving (Name things you are thankful for)

_____

_____

_____

*Pray: Lord, I thank you for waking me up this morning. I
thank you covering my family. I thank you for unity in my
home and love. I thank you for prosperity and favor.
Today, I am thanking you for _____. I will forever
give your name the praise. In Jesus name, Amen.*

Evening Thanksgiving (Thank him for what he has done
today)

_____

_____

_____

_____

Take 5 minutes and just praise/worship him
Prayer Request or Praise Report Log

DAY 14

"Whatever you do in word or deed, do all in the name of the Lord Jesus, giving thanks through Him to God the Father." Colossians 3:17

Morning Thanksgiving (Name things you are thankful for)

_____

_____

_____

Pray: Lord, I thank you for waking me up this morning. I thank you for grace. I thank for your light shining in my life, so that when people see me they see you. I thank you that I am a new creature and old things have passed away. Today, I'm thanking you for _____. I will forever give your name the praise. In Jesus name, Amen.

Evening Thanksgiving (Thank him for what he has done today)

_____

_____

_____

_____

Take 5 minutes and just praise/worship him

Prayer Request or Praise Report Log

DAY 15

"but thanks be to God, who gives us the victory through our Lord Jesus Christ."1 Corinthians 15:57

Morning Thanksgiving (Name things you are thankful for)

_____

_____

_____

Pray: Lord, I thank you for waking me up this morning. I thank you my life being filled with your glory. I thank you that miracles are happening daily for me. I thank you! Today, I'm thanking you for _____. I will forever give your name the praise. In Jesus name, Amen.

Evening Thanksgiving (Thank him for what he has done today)

_____

_____

_____

_____

Take 5 minutes and just praise/worship him

Prayer Request or Praise Report Log

Use This Section To Begin Your Journal

of the

UNLEASHING
Of
Supernatural Miracles
And
Unexplainable Blessings In Your Life

_____

_____

_____

_____

_____

_____

_____

_____

_____

_____

_____

_____

_____

_____

_____

_____

_____

_____

_____

_____

_____

_____

_____

_____

For more information or to sow into our ministry:

Sharon Hall-Green
3226 Norwich Street
Brunswick, GA 31523
www.shayministries.com
CashApp: $Shayministries

Made in the USA
Columbia, SC
25 May 2020